HIGH CALL to Pray

CAPAZIN THORNTON

High Call to Pray / by Capazin Thornton
Copyright © *2013*
ISBN: 978-0-9755473-0-4

Printed by CreateSpace

Cover design by Cathi Stevenson
Front cover image © 2013, Vasily Pindyurin /Bigstock.com

Available from Amazon.com, CreateSpace.com,
and other retail outlets
To learn more about and/or request other publications
by Capazin Thornton, please visit the website:
www.capazin.com

Lovingly dedicated to the Body of Christ,
and to my children, Zarie and James,
and my grandsons, Cameron, Mitchel, and Morgan

CONTENTS

CONTENTS (continued)

Introduction

Throughout the Bible, we see God's people joining with Him through prayer to accomplish His will in the earth.

For instance, the prophet Elijah was raised up by God to counter the evil spiritual climate created by Israel's wicked King Ahab and Queen Jezebel. Elijah stood against and defeated eight hundred fifty idol worshipping false prophets. The Bible says, "Elijah was a man with a nature like ours, and he prayed earnestly that it would not rain; and it did not rain on the land for three years and six months. And He prayed again, and the heaven gave rain, and the earth produced its fruit." (Jas 5:17, 18; 1 Ki 16:30-33; 18:19)

There are examples of people asking God for their heart's desire, while the thing prayed for was precisely what God desired to fulfill His purpose.

Hannah's earnest prayer

Hannah prayed and vowed if God would bless her and Elkanah to have a son she would give him back to serve the Lord all the days of His life. God answered Hannah's prayer, fulfilling her deep maternal longing. More importantly, in Hannah's son Samuel, God ultimately had a mouthpiece and channel of light to declare His Word to a perverse generation. For, "the word of the Lord was rare in those days, there was no widespread revelation" (1 Sam 3:1).

When Samuel was weaned, Hannah took him to live in the temple and be trained for the priesthood by Eli the priest. Although Eli was not the best role model because he failed to discipline his own sons, "Samuel grew, and the Lord was with him and let none of his words fall to the ground" (1 Sam 3:19). Samuel became and remained a faithful judge, priest, prophet, and intercessor for God's people all the days of his life. What a fantastic example of God answering the prayers of ordinary people!

Anticipation of Messiah's advent

Even though Jesus Christ, God's glorious Son throughout eternity, divested Himself of all His divine splendor and glory to become human, born of a woman according to God's timetable, people like the devout Simeon and the prophetess Anna recognized the signs of Messiah's coming because they were people of consistent prayer. (Jn 1:1, 14; Phil 2:5-8; Gal. 4:4; Lk 2:25-38)

Outpouring of the Holy Spirit

After His resurrection and before ascending back to Heaven, Christ directed His disciples to wait in Jerusalem until they were ". . . endued with power from on high." While they waited, they prayed. For ten days about one hundred twenty disciples ". . . continued with one accord in prayer and supplication" until the mighty outpouring of the Holy Spirit on the Day of Pentecost. (Lk 24:49; Acts 1:14; 2:1-4; Joel 2:28)

Certainly God sent the Holy Spirit according to His sovereign plan and promise. Yet, the disciples' earnest prayers created an atmosphere of faith and expectation for the Holy Spirit's arrival. Through the partnership of Almighty God with consecrated, praying Christ believers, the New Testament church was birthed in power.

Call to every generation

The church's purpose is to magnify the Lord so that His glory (majesty, splendor, honor, greatness and power) fill the earth. God says, "but truly, as I live, all the earth shall be filled with the glory of the Lord" (Num 14:21).

God's people in every generation have a mandate to seek God and bring the righteous policies of Heaven to bear in the earth. While preaching the good news of salvation through Jesus Christ and making disciples of all nations is the goal, the "effective fervent prayers of the righteous" (Jas 5:16) are the fundamental means to prepare the way for the preaching and teaching of God's burden-removing, yoke-destroying Word.

Through faith-filled, heartfelt and fervent prayer, tremendous power is released to break through spiritual barriers, destroy demonic strongholds, and open doors for the entrance of God's Word.

HIGH CALL TO PRAY was written to ignite in you a passion to pray and help you develop and maintain a dynamic, focused prayer life.

May God's richest blessings be yours as you stand up in the Spirit, fully clothed with the armor of God, and respond to the high call to pray!

Capazin Thornton

1

Prayer Defined

Over the centuries many gifted men and women have written books on prayer, teaching from the Word of God and sharing inspirational stories to motivate God's people to pray with confidence and expectation. Some have defined prayer simply as talking to God and listening when He talks back. Others expound upon different kinds of prayer (such as confession, petitions, intercessions, consecration, thanksgiving, praise, and worship).

In my personal search to understand more about prayer, the Holy Spirit led me to the Greek word *koinonia* (koy-nohn-ee'ah), which is wonderfully explosive with prayer meaning. Koinonia is translated into English as *communication, fellowship, participation, partnership, contribution, communion,* and *distribution*. Each of these words is useful to reveal dynamic aspects of prayer.

Prayer is Communication with God

> To communicate is to *speak, declare, voice, reveal, unveil, proclaim, pronounce, make known, transmit information, converse, informally visit, impart or interchange thoughts, have heart-to-heart chats.*

God speaks to us

God speaks through His written Word

The primary way God speaks to us is through the Bible. The original manuscripts were breathed out by God, a process where Spirit-moved men produced Spirit-breathed writings. (2 Tim 3:16; 2 Pet 1:21) Thousands of copies were handwritten on papyrus, later on parchment, and ultimately onto paper. Today, this miraculously powerful and supernaturally preserved book has been translated into multiple languages so that people all over the world can access and know God's Word for themselves.

Speaking out from the pages of the Holy Scriptures, God reveals Himself, unveils His plan for our lives, and gives us valuable information, illustrations, and instructions to live by. Through the Bible, God progressively comes out from behind the curtain of invisibility, ultimately showing Himself and speaking through His Son Jesus Christ, who is the *brightness* (outshining) *of His glory* and the *express image* of His person. (Heb 1:3)

Prayer and the Bible go hand-in-hand. As we read God's Word, we can discover a great deal about the heart, mind, and will of God. We can search out and lay hold to His "exceedingly great and precious promises" (2 Pet 1:4). Then, when we pray, we can ask God to meet needs according to what He has already promised in His written Word.

The Bible is indeed the solution book for the challenges we face every day. It provides practical wisdom for godly living in every age because, "The counsel of the Lord stands forever, the plans of His heart to all generations" (Ps 33:11).

If we do not understand how to apply Scripture to a given situation, we can pray to God for wisdom. God promises to graciously respond: "If any of you lacks wisdom, let him ask of God, who gives to all liberally and without reproach, and it will be given to him" (Jas 1:5). The fact is, every time we read the Bible we should expect God to speak to our hearts and illuminate our minds with wisdom from above.

God speaks to the inner man

The Bible reveals that man is essentially three parts in one. He is a spirit, with a soul, housed in a body. The apostle Paul refers to the human spirit as the *inner man*. The apostle Peter calls it the *hidden person of the heart*. (1 Thess 5:23; Eph 3:16; 1 Pet 3:4)

Before faith in Christ, all are spiritually dead—separated from the life of God and dominated by the law of sin and death. (Eph 2:1; Rom 5:12) However, the moment a person receives Christ as Savior, he or she is spiritually regenerated by the power of the Holy Spirit and becomes a *new creation*. It is in the recreated human spirit that the Holy Spirit takes up residence. The Holy Spirit then bears witness with the believer's spirit that he or she is a child of God. (Jn 3:6; Tit 3:5; 2 Cor 5:17; Jn 14:16-17; Rom 8:16)

Revelations from the Holy Spirit

The Holy Spirit continues to work within the spirit of the Christ believer to unveil God's desires, "For it is God who works in you both to will and to do for His good pleasure" (Phil 2:13).

It is essential to understand that the revelations of God and movements of the Holy Spirit take place in the Christ believer's spirit. Therefore believers must learn to be sensitive to the witness, voice, wooing, leading, and constraints of the Holy Spirit within.

The sound of His voice in the inner man

Most often God speaks to one's spirit in a still small voice, as He did to the prophet Elijah (1 Ki 19:12). Sometimes an audible voice is heard as in the case of the apostles Peter and Paul (Acts 10:13; 9:4). God speaks to our hearts to bring clarity, confirmation, correction, and encouragement. Great peace, joy, and hope result from hearing and obeying God's voice.

In order to clearly hear God's voice in one's spirit, one's soul (mind, will, and emotions) must be still. Our souls must be trained to be spirit ruled and not sense ruled. Whenever my soul tries to magnify the circumstances above God, I command it to be silent and to wait patiently for God to speak, just as it is written in the Psalms:

> "My soul, wait silently for God alone, for my expectation is from Him. He only is my rock and my salvation; He is my defense; I shall not be moved." (Ps 62:5-6)

> "Surely I have calmed and quieted my soul, like a weaned child with his mother; like a weaned child is my soul within me." (Ps 131:2)

Once a holy hush comes over the soul, one can more clearly hear God speaking within. As God's children born of His Spirit, we can know our Heavenly Father's voice just as easily as a natural child comes to recognize and know his daddy's voice.

We can communicate with God

Comfortably, effortlessly, spontaneously

God wants his children to communicate with Him any time, any place. Nehemiah prayed within himself to God for an answer while standing in the presence of King Artaxerxes (Neh 2:4). When Hannah desired a child, she communicated from her heart to God, through tears and anguish of soul, "... only her lips moved, but her voice was not heard ..." (1 Sam 1:13). God granted the desire of Hannah's heart. After the birth and dedication of her son Samuel, Hannah thanked the Lord through a very enthusiastic and joyful song (1 Sam 2:1-10).

Whether we pray softly, within ourselves, or with a loud voice, on our knees, lying in bed, sitting, or standing, Christ believers should talk to God as comfortably, effortlessly, and spontaneously as one does the closest of friends.

Regarding one's own needs

We can petition God when we have a need. God promises, "...that if we ask anything according to His will, He hears us. And if we know that He hears us, whatever we ask, we know that we have the petitions that we have asked of Him" (1 Jn 5:14-15).

For the needs of others

We can intercede in prayer for people all around us who have needs. Multitudes need to be introduced to Christ the Savior. Many need deliverance, healing, and restoration. Still others need to discover their true purpose, potential, and destiny in Christ.

The prayer of one person living in right relationship and fellowship with God is very powerful. James 5:16 says: "Confess your trespasses to one another and pray for one another, that you may be healed. The effective, fervent prayer of a righteous man avails much."

Unceasing communication

Our Daddy God loves and cherishes each one of us. How he delights when we stay in constant communication with Him and freely bring our requests to Him.

Prayer is Fellowship with God

Fellowship is *companionship, togetherness,* and *friendship.*

True fellowship involves keeping company with others who hold the same things in common. The basis of a Christian's fellowship with God and one another is Christ Jesus. When we receive Christ as Savior, we enter into a living spiritual union with God and have immediate access and liberty to fellowship with Him anytime day or night.

Walk in light

However, the basis of unbroken fellowship with God is to "walk in the light as He is in the light" (1 Jn 1:7). Light speaks of the indescribable splendor, radiance, and glory of God. "God is light, pure light; there's not a trace of darkness in him" (1 Jn 1:5, MSG). To walk in light is to live in close fellowship with God, with minds renewed and hearts purified by the Word and Spirit of God. It is walking in the revelation of new creation glory, truth, righteousness, holiness, and love.

When we sin, we break fellowship with God. Our relationship with Him does not change. God is still our Father and we are still His children. However, sin will interrupt our fellowship with Him.

In order for fellowship to be restored, we must confess our sins. God promises, "If we confess our sins, He is faithful and just to forgive us our sins and to cleanse us from all unrighteousness" (1 Jn 1:9). Once sin is dealt with, we can resume and enjoy sweet fellowship with God.

Prayer is Communion with God

> Communion, derived from com, *come together* and union, *at one,* means *a blending together as one.*

Communion speaks of an intimate personal relationship marked by love, warmth, tenderness, affection, deep friendship, respect, and trust. Intimacy develops over time as the result of fellowship, heart-to-heart exchanges, sharing, and spontaneous, unreserved communication.

There were people in the Old Testament who had remarkable communion with God. Three standouts are Enoch, Abraham, and Moses.

Enoch, the pure in heart

Enoch lived during very wicked times. Yet,

because he stayed in communion with God, he was uncontaminated by the evil influences around him.

In fact, Enoch was so precious to God that God simply took him out of the earth. "By faith Enoch was translated that he should not see death; and was not found, because God had translated him: for before his translation he had this testimony, that he pleased God" (Heb 11:5).

Abraham, friend of God

Abraham is called the "friend of God" because he unconditionally believed God. With childlike faith, Abraham simply took God at His Word.

Over the course of many years, God revealed Himself to Abraham as the "Lord, God Most High, the Possessor of heaven and earth," as Abraham's "Shield," his "Exceedingly Great Reward," as Yahweh Yireh, "The Lord who sees to it and provides," and as "Almighty God." Ultimately, Abraham came to know God as the utmost promise maker and promise keeper.

Moses, seeker of intimacy with God

Moses had many close encounters with God. King David celebrated Moses' relationship with God in a song, "He made known His ways to Moses, His acts to the children of Israel" (Ps 103:7).

Moses had a profound holy respect for God and yearned for more than displays of God's miraculous power. He was interested in becoming as intimately acquainted with God as humanly possible.

On one occasion, Moses beseeched God, "Now therefore, I pray, if I have found grace in Your sight, show me now Your way, that I may know You and that I may find grace in Your sight. And consider that this nation is Your people" (Ex 33:13). God thought highly of Moses, for He spoke to Moses "face to face as a man speaks to his friend" (Ex 33:11a).

In Pursuit of Christ

Without a doubt, the greatest pursuit in life is to know and fellowship with God, which quest begins the moment we receive Christ into our hearts and are regenerated by the Holy Spirit. That is when a brilliant light comes on inside and we become aware of a glorious, joyful, peaceful new dimension of life and activity in God.

We can learn many things from reading and hearing His Word. To truly become intimately acquainted with God, however, requires spending consecrated time in His presence in adoring worship, in quiet reflection in His Word, and in listening to hear His voice when He speaks to our hearts. As we continually delight ourselves in Him and endeavor to be sensitive to the Holy Spirit, communion results.

Prayer is Participation with God

Participation is *having a part in, playing a part in, joining in,* and *sharing.*

18

Christ believers are joint heirs with Christ to the immeasurable riches of God's grace (Rom 8:17). Our Heavenly Father delights to share with us out of His treasury of infinite knowledge and wisdom.

God spoke to Jeremiah, "Call to Me, and I will answer you, and show you great and mighty things, which you do not know" (Jer 33:3). These wondrous things are naturally *un-gettable*, beyond reach, inaccessible, too lofty to know apart from divine revelation.

The good news is that God gives Christ believers understanding of the Scriptures and reveals great and mighty things to us by his Spirit. "Now we have received, not the spirit of the world, but the Spirit who is from God, that we might know the things that have been freely given to us by God" (1 Cor 2:12).

There are times our spirits may be more sensitive to the revelations of God than others. Personally, I find that hearing God's voice speak to my spirit is easiest first thing in the morning after I awake when all is still, or right after praying in the Spirit for a few minutes, or during and after prayer and fasting. During these times, fresh rays of divine light penetrate through confusing thoughts. Understanding comes. Creative ideas burst forth.

God shares divine secrets with humble, reverential, truth seekers. And, just as God promised the children of Israel, "The secret things belong to the Lord our God, but those things which are revealed belong to us and to our children forever . . ." (Deut 29:29).

Prayer is Partnership with God

> A partnership is a *collaboration*; a *co-partnership*. It involves teaming up, joining forces, merging, and uniting together.

Prayer is a partnership wherein God is the omniscient, omnipotent, and omnipresent General Partner, and we are the finite limited partners who must depend on Him. Therefore, it is God's plan, not ours, which must become the focus of our prayers.

Since God is eternally self-existing and all sufficient, it is His knowledge, understanding, wisdom, and direction that we need. And, frankly, when we ask for things, they should be the things necessary to help us become more like Him, to bless others, and to effectively fulfill what He has called us to do.

God wants us to intercede in prayer for people to receive salvation. He has already said in His Word that it is not His will that any perish but that all come to repentance and the knowledge of His Son. (2 Pet 3:9) And, He has already paid the price for all to do so. Yet, each person has to decide whether to accept or reject God's gift of salvation.

While God does not violate anyone's free will, the prayers of the righteous can be effective to get people to the right place and in the right state of heart and mind to receive the good news of salvation through Jesus Christ.

Prayer is a Contribution

> Contribute means to *make an offering,
> give together for a common purpose, give
> a share, to help, advance, promote, supply.*

God is divine, perfect, and complete in Himself. We can add nothing to Him or His works. We can, however, present ourselves as holy, living sacrifices (Rom 12:1), "an offering and a sacrifice to God for a sweet-smelling aroma" (Eph 5:2).

We bless God when we "enter His gates with thanksgiving and into His courts with praise" (Ps 100:4). When we are ". . . thankful to Him, and bless His Holy Name," we join an innumerable company of the heavenly host who praise God day and night. (Rev 5:11-12)

God always contributes to us. When we present ourselves to Him as yielded vessels, thoroughly forgetting about ourselves and concentrating on Him, as we linger in His wonderful presence, God touches our lives with fresh, tender mercies. He fills us anew with His boundless love, perfect peace, glorious joy, and mighty empowering strength.

Prayer results in Distribution

> Distribution is a *giving out, sowing,* and
> *broadcasting.*

In this dispensation of God's super amazing grace,

God wants Christ believers to sow words of life and for our lives to be good seed sown wherever He sends us. "The voice of salvation and rejoicing is in the tents of the righteous" (Ps 118:15).

Through Spirit-led prayers of intercession, God is sending us into every nation to prepare the way for the preaching of the good news of salvation and the availability of a brand new life in, by, and through Christ Jesus.

Prayer truly has many aspects. Each day we have countless opportunities to communicate, fellowship, and commune with our Heavenly Father. God loves our heartfelt expressions of praise. It pleases Him when we ask and thank Him in faith for meeting our needs according to His riches in glory by Christ Jesus. He is delighted when we entreat His mercy on behalf of others.

Beloved, God has given those cleansed by the blood of Jesus Christ an open invitation to enter into His throne room anytime day or night to freely communicate with Him in any number of ways. "Let us therefore come boldly to the throne of grace, that we may obtain mercy and find grace to help in time of need" (Heb 4:16).

2

Purpose of Prayer

The purpose of prayer is to know God and then to make Him known to others.

To Know God

God wants us to know Him, personally and intimately. He wants us to know His will for our lives. God desires:

- "that Christ may dwell in your hearts through faith . . . " (Eph 3:17a);

- " . . . that you, being rooted and grounded in love, may be able to comprehend with all the saints what is the width and length and depth and height—to know the love of Christ which passes knowledge" (Eph 3:17b-19a);

- "The eyes of your understanding being enlightened, that you may know what is the hope of His calling" (Eph 1:18a);

- "what are the riches of the glory of His inheritance in the saints, what is the exceeding greatness of His power toward us who believe . . ." (Eph 1:18b-19);

- " . . . that you may be filled with all the fullness of God" (Eph 3:19);

- " . . . that you may be filled with the knowledge of His will in all wisdom and spiritual understanding" (Col 1:9b);

- "that you may have a walk worthy of the Lord, fully pleasing Him, being fruitful in every good work and increasing in the knowledge of God" (Col 1:10).

Wow! What powerful revelations from the Spirit of God. God wants us to know Him personally through Christ. He wants Christ to live in our hearts by faith. He wants His love, His will, His wisdom, and His power to live in us. He wants the Body of Christ to be filled with all the fullness of God!

Through the miraculous, transforming power of the Word of God and the ongoing work of the Holy Spirit within us, these things will become a reality in our lives. It is the Holy Spirit's responsibility to conform us into Christ's image. It is ours to yield to the Holy Spirit and to read, meditate, study, and obey God's Word.

Through faith, we can access the superabundant grace of God. And, through faith and patience we will inherit the gracious promises of God.

Finally, it is crucial that we stay in sweet fellowship with God, that we love one another and "pray always with all prayer and supplication in the spirit, being watchful to this end with all perseverance for all the saints" (Eph 6:18).

Friends, there is absolutely nothing in life more important than developing a personal intimate relationship with God and pursuing His purpose. The apostle Paul put it aptly:

> "Yet indeed I also count all things loss for the excellence of the knowledge of Christ Jesus My Lord . . . that I may know Him and the power of His resurrection, and the fellowship of His sufferings, being conformed to His death." (Phil 3:8, 10)

To Make Him Known

The more we know Christ Jesus, the more we want to introduce Him to everyone we know. When we know Him, we realize that the goal of our praying is not to gain things, but to apprehend Christ. It is to help effect His righteous and loving rule over our individual families and over all the families of the earth, "For God is the King of all the earth . . ." (Ps 47:7).

Every Christ believer should continually delight in the God of our salvation. And, for us, communicating with our Heavenly Father should be as natural as breathing. What a joy and privilege to know Him. What an honor to be an ambassador for Christ, commissioned to make Him known throughout the world.

Becoming a House of Prayer

A personal relationship wherein we can fellowship, commune, communicate, participate, and partner with the Creator of heaven and earth is the greatest privilege afforded mankind. As the result, prayer should not be so much something we do, but what we are becoming. Individually and corporately God is calling every Christ believer to become a house of prayer for all nations. (Isa 56:7b)

3

Priority of Prayer

God wants to enrich our lives in every way. Many times, however, we fail to experience God's rich blessings because we do not have our priorities right. A priority is that which is first in order of importance. God says, "But seek first the kingdom of God and His righteousness, and all these things shall be added to you" (Mt 6:33). As we seek first God's kingdom and His righteousness, God sees to it that our needs are met.

Pray in Every Situation

Jesus said, "Men ought to pray and not to faint" (Lk 18:1). In difficult situations, we can faint, or we can pray. To faint means *to lose heart, lose strength, cave in*, or *collapse.* In other words one becomes overwhelmed and gives up in the face of seemingly insurmountable circumstances. Do not faint, lose heart, or give up. Instead, pray!

God says, "Be anxious for nothing, but in everything by prayer and supplication, with thanksgiving, let your requests be made known to God" (Phil 4:6). God is All-Powerful, All Knowing, and All Wise. He can arrest the development of any adverse circumstance. And, He knows how to get people the help they need.

God will strengthen us. He will help us. He will uphold us. He will make all things work together for good for those who love Him and are the called according to His purpose. We must have unshakable faith in God at all times. (Isa 41:10; Rom 8:28; Mk 11:22)

People with a Prayer Priority

In the Bible the real kingdom *movers and shakers*, if you will, were those whose first priority was daily worship, fellowship, and communion with God. While there are many examples of people praying, I believe those most demonstrating a habit of prayer are Jesus of Nazareth, Paul the apostle, Nehemiah, and King David.

Jesus of Nazareth

Christ of eternity was manifest in the flesh as Jesus of Nazareth, born of the Virgin Mary who miraculously conceived Him by the power of the Holy Spirit. On earth Jesus divested Himself of divine privilege and power, depending instead upon God the Father who anointed Him with the Holy Ghost and with power.

Most times we think of Jesus' earthly ministry in terms of His amazing works of casting out demons, opening blind eyes, healing the incurable, and raising the dead. We love to focus on His powerful sermons, engaging parables, and miraculous deeds. We tend to overlook the fact that behind His dynamic public ministry was a private life of consistent prayer.

Jesus taught His disciples to pray by precept and example. He freely communicated with and stayed in constant fellowship with God the Father. Mark's Gospel says, "Now in the morning, having risen a long while before daylight, He went out and departed to a solitary place; and there He prayed" (Mk 1:35). Luke writes that Jesus went up into a mountain and ". . . continued all night in prayer" (Lk 6:12). John records the Lord's Prayer where he prayed for Himself, His disciples, and all believers. (Jn 17)

As the result of staying in communion with Father God and yielding to and relying on the Holy Spirit, Jesus Christ found the fortitude and strength to endure incomprehensible suffering and a gruesome death on the cross, all for our sins. Christ Jesus is the best example of one who prayed at all times and completely trusted and submitted to the will of God the Father.

Paul the Apostle

The most prominent "pray-er" in the New Testament is the apostle Paul. His letters are full of prayers, thanksgiving, and praise. This apostle did not just talk about prayer, nor did he simply write about it. He did not merely exhort others to pray. Paul prayed heartfelt, boiling point prayers, ". . . night and day praying exceedingly" (1 Thess 3:10).

After he became a Christ believer, Paul suffered great persecution at the hands of the Jews. Five times he was severely beaten with whips and three times with rods. One time he was stoned and left for dead. He was shipwrecked three times and capsized in the sea for a night and a day. He suffered hunger, thirst, sleeplessness, fatigue, and perils by land and sea.

Yet, Paul's letters to the churches express great joy and faith in the Lord. Paul not only knew the Holy Scriptures, he knew the love and faithfulness of the God of the Scriptures. Paul found out "many are the afflictions of the righteous but the Lord delivers him out of them all" (Ps 34:19). He discovered that God's grace is sufficient. (2 Cor 12:9) Paul was a man sold out to constant, unwavering prayer.

Nehemiah

Nehemiah was consumed with a passion to see Jerusalem rebuilt. Day and night he "wept, and mourned . . . and fasted, and prayed before the God of heaven . . . for the children of Israel" (Neh 1:4, 6).

Nehemiah prayed and then asked King Artaxerxes

for leave of absence to go to Jerusalem for the purpose of rebuilding the walls and gates of the city which had been broken down and burned by the Babylonian conquerors. The king gave Nehemiah time off and also addressed letters to the keepers of the king's forest to give Nehemiah timber and to the governors in the region to permit Nehemiah to pass through to Judah.

Once in Judah, Nehemiah rallied the priests, nobles, officers, and people to rise up and build. Through fierce opposition, Nehemiah persevered and pressed through to the completion of his God inspired task. As the result of Nehemiah's prayers, leadership, hard work, and perseverance, Jerusalem experienced restoration.

King David

After hearing of the death of King Saul and Jonathan his son, David and his men mourned and fasted for Saul, Jonathan, God's people, and the house of Israel. (2 Sam 1:12) For many years David knew that he would take Saul's place as king, but he took no steps to assume that role until after he sought the Lord.

> "It happened after this that David inquired of the Lord, saying, 'Shall I go up to any of the cities of Judah?' And the Lord said to him, 'Go up.' David said, 'Where shall I go up?' And He said, 'To Hebron.' So David went up there . . ." (2 Sam 2:1-2)

To inquire literally means *to seek the face of*. David proceeded only after seeking and obtaining God's direction. Notice that God answered David clearly—yes, go up to Hebron. In Hebron, David was anointed king over the house of Judah where he reigned seven and one-half years. (2 Sam 5:5) He then reigned over all of Israel and Judah for thirty-three years.

Throughout his life, David was a genuine worshipper and a man of spontaneous, heart-felt prayer.

Pray, and then Wait on God

Always pray before making decisions, especially life-changing decisions that can affect your walk and work for the Lord. For example, suppose you hear that there is a great move of God's Spirit in another city. Unless God directs you to go somewhere else, stay put. Despite how things look in the natural, in actuality you might be just moments away from your greatest breakthrough right where you are.

The Bible says, "Trust in the Lord with all your heart, and lean not on your own understanding; in all your ways acknowledge Him, and He shall direct your paths" (Prov 3:5-6).

Getting Priorities Straight

God's priorities must become our priorities. God desires that all be saved. Let us rededicate ourselves to seize every opportunity, day and night, to passionately seek after the Lord and fervently pray, praise, and offer thanks to Him for all people. (1 Tim 2:1-4)

4

Perfect Character of God

Character can be described as the essential nature or qualities of someone, good or bad. Basic to good character is truthfulness, trustworthiness, faithfulness, integrity, and honor. While human character at best is flawed and inconsistent, God's character is perfect, exceedingly excellent, never changes, and speaks of His willingness to meet our needs.

God is Love

The central truth underlying all that God does is the fact that God is Love! The kind of love that God is by nature and that He freely pours out from Himself to us is radically different from any love previously understood by man.

Prior to Jesus of Nazareth, the most common words used in the Greek culture to define love were storge, eros, and philia.

Storge (stor'-gay) can be described as a natural affection based on kinship. While love of family is important, it is sometimes expressed in selfish and self-serving ways.

Eros (air'ohs) is a passionate love, based on sexual desire. God's plan is that a man and woman experience sexual fulfillment within marriage. (Gen 2:24)

Philia (fil-ee'-ah) means "fondness" or "friendship." It is birthed out of shared or common interests or when one finds a pleasing characteristic or attribute in another. This kind of love can be selfish, such as when friends become cliquish, excluding from association others who do not share similar interests, attributes, assets, or ambitions.

Uncommon Love

Agape (ah-ah'-pay) is used to express the essential nature of God. Unlike any other love, agape is pure, sacrificial, merciful, and unconditional. The proof of God's amazing love is this: ". . . while we were yet sinners, Christ died for us" (Rom 5:8).

Agape is a totally democratic love. God accepts each one who receives His Son, regardless of race, gender, age, or socioeconomic status. "For God so loved the world that He gave His only begotten Son, that whoever believes in Him should not perish but have everlasting life" (Jn 3:16).

Agape is a relentless, tenaciously devoted love. It is a love that always gives and seeks the highest good for the person loved. "How great is the love the Father has lavished on us, that we should be called children of God" (1 Jn 3:1).

As circumstances change, other kinds of love fizzle out. In super dynamic contrast, the everlasting God loves us with an everlasting love!

God is Good

When Moses asked to see God's glory, God responded, "The LORD, The LORD God, merciful and gracious, long-suffering, and abundant in goodness and truth, keeping mercy for thousands, forgiving iniquity and transgression and sin. . ." (Ex 34:6-7a). God's glory then is an outshining of His awesome, benevolent nature. God is merciful, gracious, long-suffering, forgiving, and abundant in goodness and truth.

God is morally excellent and perfect in every way. There is no bad in His nature or His acts. W.E. Vine wrote, "God is essentially, absolutely and consummately good." The Bible says, "The earth is full of the goodness of the Lord" (Ps 33:5).

God is always acting positively on our behalf and for our advantage. When we truly understand this, we will never give in to the urge to point an angry finger at God for the pain, misery, turmoil, poverty, sickness, and suffering in the world.

Ultimately, behind all the ills of society is "...that serpent of old, called the Devil and Satan, who deceives the whole world. . . " (Rev 12:9). He is the "thief" who comes "to kill, steal and destroy" (Jn 10:10a).

God's desire is for Christ believers to resist every temptation, ace every test, and stand victorious through every trial of life. We can overcome the obstacles we face by laying hold of and declaring Christ's victory—over the devil, the world, and sin. The Lord Jesus reminds us:

> " . . . In the world you will have tribulation; but be of good cheer, I have overcome the world." (Jn 16:33)

> "You are of God, little children, and have overcome them, because He who is in you is greater than he who is in the world." (1 Jn 4:4)

> "For whatever is born of God overcomes the world. And this is the victory that has over-come the world—our faith." (1 Jn 5:4)

Always keep in mind that God has a way of causing every circumstance to work for good in the lives of those who love God and are the called according to His purpose. (Rom 8:28)

God desires our completeness, harmony, and fulfillment. His thoughts toward us are continually good. (See Jer 29:11, AMP.)

God is Gracious, Full of Compassion

> "The Lord is gracious, and full of compassion, slow to anger, and great in mercy." (Ps 145:8)

The word gracious literally means *disposed to show favor*. The Lord's disposition is to show us favor! He loves us tenderly and is full of eager yearning to help us.

It is important to remember that God uses people to dispense His love and compassion. The Bible says the love of God has been poured out in our hearts by the Holy Spirit. We can thus express His love to others.

Years ago, my friend Dominica and I ministered at a convalescent home in Los Angeles. During the first weeks, some of the people expressed themselves through pounding on tables, yelling, and even cursing.

Besides praying, fasting, and declaring spiritual authority over demonic forces, Dominica and I continued to pour out the love of God through gracious words and deeds. Saying "Jesus loves you, and so do I" caused eyes to brighten up and smiles to break out. Before long, people were set free from spiritual chains of bitterness, hurt, and pain. After about six months, we experienced some marvelous breakthroughs. A number received healing physically, emotionally, and mentally.

When we allow the love and compassion of God to be released through us both in prayer and through gracious deeds, miracles happen and lives are changed.

God is Faithful

Throughout the ages, God has shown Himself faithful, reliable, trustworthy, true to His Word. God's faithfulness has never been based on what man does. His faithfulness to all generations is because of who He is.

> "God is not a man that He should lie, nor a son of man that He should repent. Has He said, and will He not do? Or has He spoken, and will He not make it good?" (Num 23:19)

God is not a mortal. He is the Eternal, self-existing Creator of the universe. It is impossible for God to lie. He is The Truth. And, He has magnified His Word above all His Name.

God is completely reliable and trustworthy. Most certainly, if God said it, you can count on it!

These are just a few of the extraordinarily wonderful qualities of God. When you pray, recall God's excellent, flawless character. Think about His goodness and the fact that His thoughts towards us are continually good. God is love and full of loving kindness. He is gracious and full of compassion. We do not have to beg Him. He is already disposed to show us favor. Glory to God!

Always remember that God is an awesome, benevolent God, who cannot lie, and His promises are backed by all the honor of His Name.

5

Power of Praying God's Word

"I will worship toward Your holy temple; and praise Your name, for Your lovingkindness and Your truth; For you have magnified Your word above all Your name." (Ps 138:2)

God revealed Himself to Israel as Yahweh, the eternal, self-existing God. "Hear, O Israel: The Lord [Yahweh] our God [Elohim] is one Lord [Yahweh]" (Deut 6:4). Then, in covenant relation with His people He made Himself known by various Yahweh compound names: Yahweh-Raah—"the Lord is Shepherd," Yahweh-Rapha—"the Lord is Healer," Yahweh-Yireh—"the Lord will see (to it) and provide," and so on. (*See* Ps 23:1, Ex 15:26; Gen 22:14.)

And, even though God's Name is exceedingly great, God has magnified His Word above all His Name! The universe was created and is still being upheld by God's Word. Thus, when we declare God's Word, we release the power and authority of the throne of God in Heaven into the circumstances of our lives.

God's Word is Alive

> "For the Word that God speaks is alive and full of power [making it active, operative, energizing, and effective] . . . ." (Heb 4:12, AMP)

While there are many books that can stimulate our minds and creative imaginations and inspire and motivate us, there is only one book in the universe that has power to raise the dead, to cause demons to flee, to convert a sinner's heart, and to heal, deliver, and restore broken, crushed and bruised people. That book, of course, is the Bible, the written Word of God, the revealed will of God.

Inherent in the Word is explosive, miracle-working, life giving, situation changing power. God's Word is divine seed that can supersede any negative circumstance! There is absolutely nothing too difficult for God to do or undo, ". . . For with God all things are possible" (Mk 10:27). The Word of God has supernatural power to transform your life and those for whom you pray.

God's Word is the Word of the King

"Where the word of a king is, there is power." Christ is the "King of kings and Lord of lords." Every Christ believer is a king and priest to God. As priests, we can pray and offer thanks to God for all people. As kings, we can declare God's Word, release the will of Heaven, and loose God's ruling power into the situation at hand. (Eccl 8:4; Rev 19:16; 1 Pet 2:9; Rev 1:5-6; Rev 5:10).

God's Word Discharges Light

When God created the earth, He spoke words. For instance, God said "Light be," and light came forth (Gen 1:3). Light still obeys God's voice. "For He spoke, and it was; he commanded and it stood fast" (Ps 33:9).

God is light. Thus, when God's Word is proclaimed, light is discharged. Light advances and darkness retreats.

God's Word Looses Angels

"Bless the Lord you His angels who excel in strength, who do His Word, heeding the voice of His Word." (Ps 103:20)

When God's Word goes forth, angels are released to minister on behalf of the heirs of salvation. When demonic forces are prevailed against, the heavens pour down righteousness and the earth opens up to receive salvation. (Heb 1:14; Is 45:8)

God's Word Inspires Confidence in Prayer

> "Now this is the confidence that we have in him, that, if we ask anything according to His will, He hears us. And if we know that He hears us, whatever we ask, we know that we have the petitions that we have asked of Him." (1 Jn 5:14-15)

Here we see that praying God's Word is powerful because: We can be confident that we are praying according to God's will; we know that God hears us; and we know that we have the petitions we ask of Him.

A vital key to answered prayer is found in the Gospel of Mark. God says: "...whatever things you ask when you pray, believe that you receive them, and you will have them" (Mk 11:24). If at the moment we pray we believe we receive the things we are praying for, the Word promises that we shall have those things. Thus, if we truly believe this promise, we will not keep asking God for the same thing over and over. Rather, we will thank and praise Him in faith until the thing we believe we received at the time we first prayed manifests.

Declaring God's Word Benefits Us

When we pray God's Word, we benefit spirit, soul, and body:

- The Word renews our minds. (Rom 12:2)

- The Word is health or medicine to all our flesh. (Prov 4:22)

- The Word stimulates faith in our hearts. (Rom 10:17)

Bible faith is having an unshakable confidence and trust in God and His Word. It is "the leaning of your entire human personality on Him in absolute trust and confidence in His power, wisdom and goodness." It is thinking, speaking, and acting accordingly.

God's Word Releases Joy, Love, and Peace

When we declare God's Word, especially Scriptures regarding the joy, love and peace of God, we release dynamic forces of life that have the power to lift heavy burdens and bring positive change to those for whom we pray.

God's Word is Forever

"Forever O Lord, Your Word is settled in heaven." (Ps 119:89)

Sometimes when we want to indicate that something is taking an inordinate period of time, we say that it is taking forever. Of course, we really have no earthly idea of how long forever really is.

God promises that whoever believes in Christ should not perish but have everlasting life. Everlasting life is perpetual life, that is, life without end, life that never runs out, life that is forever! How important it is for people to know Christ. For Christ believers this perpetual life is with God and full of indescribable love, joy, peace, splendor and beauty.

It is so wonderful to know that God's Word will never fade out or become obsolete. God's Word is forever established in heaven. God's Word lives and abides forever!

We can never go wrong when we pray God's Word, especially in the revelation and spirit of the New Testament. God wants us to pray with understanding. The apostle Paul wrote: "... I will also pray [intelligently] with my mind and understanding ..." (1 Cor 14:15a). To pray with understanding means to pray with purpose, intent, and design based on knowing how to apply God's Word in a given situation. It means to pray with a mind renewed, girded up, and prepared with God's Word. In other words, it means to *pray with a spiritual mind.*

When we pray according to the Word and with the help of the Holy Spirit, we can be assured that we are bringing the will of our Heavenly Father to bear in every situation over which we pray.

6

Praying in the Spirit

> For if I pray in an [unknown] tongue, my spirit [by the Holy Spirit within me] prays, but my mind is unproductive [it bears no fruit and helps nobody]. Then what am I to do? I will pray with my spirit [by the Holy Spirit that is within me], but I will also pray [intelligently] with my mind and understanding; I will sing with my spirit [by the Holy Spirit that is within me], but I will sing [intelligently] with my mind and understanding also." (1 Cor 14:14-15, AMP)

Previously, we looked at the power of praying God's Word, which is praying intelligently with the mind and understanding. Here we will look briefly at what it means to pray in the spirit.

Praying in the Spirit

Praying in the spirit literally means to *pray in the spiritual realm with the Holy Spirit's aid.*

My spirit prays

When one prays in the spirit, it is not prayer coming from one's mind or intellect. It is prayer proceeding from one's spirit or inner man.

By the Holy Spirit within me

When we pray in the spirit, the Holy Spirit helps us pray. "Likewise the Spirit also helps us in our weaknesses. For we do not know what we should pray for as we ought but the Spirit Himself makes intercession for us with groanings which cannot be uttered" (Rom 8:26)—groanings that cannot be expressed or articulated in words.

The Greek word translated helps is sunantilambano, made up of sun, *together with*, anti, *over against*, and lambano, *to take*. The word speaks of the action of a person coming to another's aid by taking hold together with that person the load he is carrying. The person helping does not take the entire load, but helps the other person.

In like manner, the Holy Spirit indwelling in us comes to our aid in prayer. He does not pray for us, He helps us to pray effectively.

Many times we do not have all the facts concerning

matters over which we are to pray. Thus, naturally speaking, it is impossible for us to know precisely what to pray in these situations. The Holy Spirit, however, knows everything. He will help us pray effectively.

Sometimes the Holy Spirit will prompt us to pray by giving us thoughts, impressions, a flash of a name or face, a word of knowledge, a word of wisdom, or a dream or vision. Other times, waking up suddenly and finding it difficult to go back to sleep is a signal to pray.

There are times when our souls are greatly overwhelmed by devastating events. Who can forget September 11, 2001 when terrorists flew airplanes into the World Trade Center in New York and thousands died? Or, hearing of devastating earthquakes and tsunamis killing thousands of people in a matter of minutes. Survivors are left homeless and lacking basic necessities. Sometimes, it is difficult to find words to express the sadness of our hearts. We may groan and cry, even vehemently. In times such as these we should rely on the Holy Spirit to strengthen us and make our prayers effective to break through oppressive atmospheres to release God's love, peace, joy, and grace.

In Different Languages

Speaking in other tongues or languages for the purpose of prayer, worship, and spiritual edification is discussed in 1 Corinthians 14, verses 2, 4, 14, and 15. Praying in tongues is simply praying in languages birthed in one's spirit or inner man by the Holy Spirit.

Praying in these languages of the spirit is powerful because:

• The Holy Spirit helps us to pray effectively in situations where we do not know the particular definite thing to pray.

• The Holy Spirit helps us pray beyond the limits of our natural minds.

• Our prayers are not hindered because of any language barrier or inability to articulate.

Through praying in languages of the spirit, we can efficiently pray for the needs of people anywhere in the world.

• We speak mysteries (divine secrets) in the spiritual realm.

• When we pray in the spirit, the Holy Spirit helps us pray the perfect will of God.

Additionally, as we pray in languages of the spirit, we benefit personally. We edify ourselves. We also receive a rest and refreshing.

Can any Christ believer pray in languages of the spirit? Yes, when filled or baptized with the Holy Spirit. The New Testament makes a distinction between being born of the Spirit (which all true believers are) and being filled with or baptized with the Holy Spirit.

In John 4:14, Jesus says that whoever drinks of the water that He gives will never thirst. But the water that He gives will become a fountain of water springing up into everlasting life. This scripture speaks of regeneration, being born again, by the work of the Holy Spirit.

Regarding the fullness of the Spirit, Jesus said, "He who believes in Me, as the Scripture has said, out of his heart will flow rivers of living water. But this He spoke concerning the Spirit, whom those believing in Him would receive; for the Holy Spirit was not yet given, because Jesus was not yet glorified" (Jn 7:38-39).

If you are a Christ believer who has not been baptized with the Holy Spirit, simply ask God to baptize you with the Holy Spirit. God promises that whoever asks shall receive. (Lk 11:9-13) Believe you receive. Open your mouth and by faith begin to speak in other languages as the Holy Spirit gives you the prompting to speak.

As you pray in other languages from your spirit, keep in mind that according to Scripture you are praying the will of God and, at the same time, you are building yourself up spiritually.

Living in the Spirit

Being filled with the Holy Spirit is far more than speaking in tongues or languages of the spirit. It means to daily live under the controlling influence of the Holy Spirit and the inexhaustible mighty power inherent in Christ.

The Holy Spirit illuminates our hearts to understand the things of God. He helps us pray and praise. He knows the mind and will of the Father. He is the Spirit of Truth. He will lead and guide us into all truth.

The Holy Spirit gives us the ability to have intimacy

with the Father. He will make Jesus Christ gloriously real in our lives. He will enable us to live a holy life and emanate the fruit of the spirit. He gives us the ability to do divine exploits for the kingdom of God. He will manifest the character, wisdom, and power of God through yielded vessels to meet human needs.

Joy in the Spirit

When one is filled with the Holy Spirit there is a greater dimension of the joy of the Lord. The Holy Spirit Himself in fact is pure joy! He is the oil of gladness. Nehemiah says, "The joy of the Lord is your strength" (Neh 8:10).

Joy can be manifested by calm, cheerful delight, or in jubilant gladness expressed through dancing and singing, or even through tears. No matter what state of mind we are in when we begin prayer, we should pray through until we sense peace and victory. Then we should end our time of prayer by releasing the powerful force of joy through heartfelt praise and thanksgiving.

We have seen that tremendous spiritual power is released when we pray the Word and when we pray in the Spirit. Truly as we yield to the Holy Spirit to pray as He desires in any given situation, we release the dynamic, miracle-working, explosive power of God into the lives of those for whom we pray.

7

Praying with God-Given Authority

Christ Has All Authority

After His resurrection and before His ascension back to heaven, the Lord Jesus proclaimed, "All authority has been given to Me in heaven and on earth" (Mt 28:18). Authority (Greek exousia) means *freedom of action* and *right to act*. Christ has absolute freedom and the right to act and exercise dominion over all creation. And, He has delegated authority to every Christ believer.

In Ephesians chapter 1 we see the ascended Christ at the right hand of God the Father:

"... He [God] raised Him [Christ] from the dead and seated Him at His right hand in the heavenly places, far above all principality and power and might and dominion, and every name that is named, not only in this age but also in that which is to come, and He put all things under His feet . . . ." (Eph 1:20-22a)

Christ is Lord over all creation in Heaven, earth, and beneath the earth. Everything in the universe is subject to His authority and rule.

Believers Have Authority in Christ

High Spiritual Position in Christ

God "raised us up together, and made us sit together in the heavenly places in Christ Jesus" (Eph 2:6). To be seated in heavenly places with Christ is to be in union with Him, to be partakers of His resurrection life, power and glory, and to have authority and dominion in the earth.

Authority Over Principalities and Powers

Our spiritual position in Christ is far above principalities and powers that operate in the lower heavens and atmosphere around us. Demonic forces are thus under our feet. That gives new meaning to: "Behold, I give you the authority to trample on serpents and scorpions, and over all the power of the enemy, and nothing by any means shall hurt you" (Lk 10:19).

Authority to Use the Name of Jesus

To pray powerfully and effectively, we must know that we are ambassadors for Christ, delegated with authority to conduct kingdom business in Christ's behalf. (2 Cor 5:20) We have the right, liberty, and privilege to use the Lord's Name to bring His will to bear in the earth. In His Name, we have authority to cast out demons, heal the sick, to undo heavy burdens, and set spiritual captives free. We have the authority to release God's love, joy and peace into people's lives.

Example of Authority in Action

Praying for the sick is an area of ministry that is particularly enjoyable because many times the result of one's prayers manifests right away.

I recall a particular young man in Los Angeles named Gary who fell into a coma after suffering critical head injuries when thrown from his motorcycle. A week after the accident, a co-worker told me that the doctor's prognosis for Gary was not good—he might not survive; even if he did there would likely be some brain damage. My co-worker also told me that only Gary's immediate family could visit him in the hospital.

After hearing this report, I went into a private room to pray for Gary, something like this:

"Holy Father, I come to you in Name of

Jesus, the name that is above every name. Lord, I acknowledge and worship you as the Creator, the giver and sustainer of all life. Father, you said in your Word that it was not your will that any perish, but that all come to repentance and the knowledge of your Son. Father God, I'm asking you to extend your great mercy to Gary and forgive all his sins. I pray that Gary will not die, but will live to declare the glory of God. Lord, let him live that he may fulfill the purpose you have for his life.

Lord, I pray that Gary be loosed from the grip of death and that the same Spirit who raised Christ Jesus from the dead will quicken Gary's mortal body and raise him up out of this coma. May Gary awake to righteousness and sin no more. Thank you, Father, for your tender mercies that cover Gary's life. Amen."

When I finished praying, I knew in my spirit that Gary would recover. It was Friday afternoon. Because I no longer sensed urgency, I decided to wait until Sunday to see him in the hospital. Even though I was not a member of Gary's family, I felt certain that the Lord would give me access to see him.

I went to the hospital ICU that Sunday. When I asked at the nurses' station for directions to Gary's room, a nurse graciously directed me. When I looked into Gary's room, he was lying in the bed wide-awake with several people around him. Gary looked at me and smiled. Then one of the ladies came out of his room to talk with me.

She was Gary's girlfriend. I told her Gary and I worked on the same floor, and that Friday I had prayed for him to come out of the coma. She said Gary came out of the coma late Friday night or early Saturday morning. She told me I was welcome to go in to see him.

When I went in the room, Gary said, "hello." I asked him if he knew who I was. He said, "Sure, Capazin, I know you." We chatted for a few minutes. Then I told Gary that a group of us had prayed for him earlier in the day and that I brought a handkerchief we had all laid hands on and prayed over. I told him we believed that when the cloth was put on his body God's power would be released to heal him completely. Gary welcomed the prayer cloth.

I have not seen Gary since that day. When he got out of the, he went to work for another firm. A few months later, however, I received a letter from Gary and his girlfriend. They said they knew Gary was alive and well because of my prayers. They also said that before the accident they lived pretty much as they saw fit, but now they were going to spend the rest of their lives pursuing the Lord and His purpose. Glory to God!

Sometimes when you tell people stories like these, they rebut by telling you about someone they knew who was sick and died after being prayed for by every major healing evangelist in the country. We need

God's wisdom to lovingly respond to people in these instances.

Most importantly, we must never exalt experiences in life above the eternal Word of God. The fact is, only God knows what is in another person's heart. We must always remember that God's Word is true, whether or not we believe it and whether or not we experience what is promised.

Covenant of Great Authority and Power

The New Covenant is the Last Will and Testament of Jesus Christ and is established on better, more excellent, and more powerful promises than those given to the saints under the Old Covenant. The New Covenant includes forgiveness of sins, a new spirit, a new life in Christ, a position of right-standing (righteousness) with God, authority in Jesus' name, sonship, sanctification, glorification, eternal life, healing and health in this life, and many "exceeding great and precious promises."

God wants His children to read the Will and find out what belongs to us in, by, and through Christ. Once we lay hold to these promises by faith and bind them to our hearts, we will be able to pray in any situation with confidence, authority, and power.

> "Behold, I give you the authority to trample on serpents and scorpions, and over all the power of the enemy, and nothing by any means shall hurt you." (Lk 10:19)

56

8

Patience

In the Greek New Testament, there are two words translated patience. One, makrothumia (mak-rot-oo-mee'ah), is part of the fruit of the recreated spirit (Gal 5:23). It means *long-suffering, bearing long with, forbearing.* It relates to our attitude towards people—putting up with the frailties and offences of others without complaining.

The other word is hupomone (hoop-om-on-ay'), which is a discipline of the soul. It means *perseverance, persistence,* and *cheerful endurance* through difficult circumstances. It involves having a tenacious, hang tough, *I will not be moved attitude* that results in the power to wait for the desired result, while maintaining a cheerful attitude throughout the process.

In prayer, we need the fruit of the spirit to suffer

long with people as well as discipline of the soul to persevere through adverse circumstances of life with a cheerful attitude.

Dealing with delay

As you may have learned, sometimes the people you pray for and the circumstances you pray to change get worse before they get better. Most of us have encountered periods of intense resistance when it seems as though the heavens are shut up and the people prayed for are moving farther away than ever from receiving salvation and restoration.

After you pray for someone, do not judge the fruit of your prayer by what you see on a day-to-day basis. Keep your focus on the Lord and His Word. Realize that in the realm of the spirit changes are taking place. In fact, changes begin to take place the moment a Christ believer prays in faith. (1 Jn 5:14-15)

Sometimes delay can be caused by demonic interference such as seen in Daniel chapter 10. In the final analysis, however, God is in charge. He will work out the details and timing that will provide the greatest benefit to us, while at the same time maximize the glory He receives.

During the time between praying the promise and the manifestation of the promise, we must continue to thank and praise God on behalf of the people for whom we pray.

Suppose you prayed for someone to receive

salvation. At the time you prayed, you believed God heard and answered your prayer. You do not need to ask God again to save that person. Simply thank Him for his or her salvation.

> "Father, thank you that you sent your Word to redeem _____ ' life from destruction. Thank you that the Holy Spirit rests on _____ and is ever turning _____ ' heart to you. Thank you for your ministering spirits watching over and protecting _____ from any hurt or harm. Thank you that _____ is hungering and thirsting after righteousness..."

Works in progress

When I think of God's work in a person's life, I am reminded of the construction of a building. It is amazing to see a beautifully finished project sometimes just weeks after seeing a big empty hole in the ground.

First is excavation and hauling away tons of dirt. Next, a concrete foundation is laid. This is an extremely important phase since the foundation bears the weight of the entire structure. If the foundation is not properly laid, the building could later collapse. The higher the building, the deeper the foundation must be.

Soon we see the framework, roof, windows and doors. Then interior work such as plumbing, electrical wiring, insulation, sheetrock, painting, and putting in floors takes place. What an amazing amount of work to get from the blueprint to the finished building.

With respect to people, God constructs them from the inside out. Therefore, none of us can know the inner workings and dealings of God in another's life. For that matter, many times we do not understand what God is doing in our own lives.

Already perfected in Christ

From God's point of view, every Christ believer is already perfected in, by, and through Christ. "Moreover whom He foreknew, He also predestined to be conformed to the image of His Son that He might be the firstborn among many brethren. Moreover whom He predestined, these He also called, whom He called, these He also justified; and whom He justified, these He also glorified" (Rom 8:29-30).

Therefore, beloved, let us continue to love and suffer long with the people whom God has assigned us to live with, work with, and pray for. And, let us continue to thank and praise Him for His work in their lives, as well as our own.

The Lord is gracious

When it seems as though it is taking forever to see results, be patient and remember:

> "The Lord will wait, that He may be gracious to you; and therefore He will be exalted that He may have mercy on you. For the Lord is a God of justice; blessed are all those who wait for Him." (Is 30:18)

9

Praise

We were created to proclaim and show forth the excellent virtues of the God and Father of our Lord and Savior Jesus Christ. We were made to acclaim, applaud, boast about, congratulate, extol, magnify, glorify, celebrate, and salute the Lord who is exceedingly great and exceedingly greatly to be praised now and forevermore for all that He has done for us.

Many know they should praise God, but feel limited in their expression of praise to Him. There are a number of Hebrew words used throughout the book of Psalms translated into English simply as praise. Taking a closer look at these words and their meanings will help us better understand and implement more expressions of praise to the Lord.

The Book of Psalms was used for praying, singing,

and reciting in the worship services in the temple in Jerusalem. We will look at seven of these dynamic expressions of praise that we can use in our individual times of praise as well as in corporate worship service.

Expressions of Praise

Yadah

Yadah (yaw-dah) means *to praise with extended hands, throw up the hands, to re-vere or worship with extended hands, give thanks, thanksgiving.*

David said, "I will praise [yadah] You with my whole heart" (Ps 138:1). When we extend our hands upward toward God in heaven, it outwardly expresses a heart full of gratitude, love, and reverence for Him. Truly, we should ". . . give thanks [yadah] at the remembrance of His holiness" (Ps 30:4b). Whether alone or in a corporate setting, stretching our hands toward heaven is a good starting point to express praise to God.

Towdah

Towdah (tow-dah) is *an extension of the hands in adoration and thanksgiving, con-fession, (sacrifice of) praise, thanksgiving, thank offering.*

In Psalm 100, worshippers are exhorted: "Enter

into His gates with thanksgiving [towdah] and into His courts with praise . . ." (Ps 100:4).

Towdah is different from yadah in that it is a *sacrifice of praise*. It is an offering of thanks in the midst of and despite difficult circumstances.

Even if my body is racked with pain, I will thank and praise the Lord because He is my Healer.

Even though my bank account may be down to zero, I will thank God for being my Provider.

Even when I have been done horribly wrong, I will praise God for His forgiving grace, goodness, loving kindness, and tender mercies towards me as well as to the one who did me wrong.

The sacrifice of praise is "the fruit of our lips giving thanks to His name" (Heb 15:13). The fact is, we should pray God continually no matter what the circumstances.

First Thessalonians 5:16-18 says: "Rejoice always, pray without ceasing, in everything give thanks; for this is the will of God in Christ Jesus for you." Giving thanks in everything is the highest expression of faith and is the will of God for you and me.

Halal

Halal (haw-lal') means to *make a jubilant sound* and *celebrate*.

One of the functions of the Old Testament priests was "to stand every morning to thank and praise [halal] the Lord, and likewise at evening" (1 Chron 23:30). The word hallelujah comes from halal, and is literally a command: All of you must praise Jah!

Halal is also translated boast. "My soul shall make her boast in the Lord" (Ps 34:2). "In God we boast all the day long" (Ps 44:8). Halal is a joyful, exuberant and triumphant expression of praise of the greatness of God and His glorious Name.

In the New Testament Mary says, "My soul magnifies the Lord and my spirit has rejoiced in God my Savior" (Lk 1:46-47). The NEB Bible translates it this way: "tell out my soul the greatness of God." Notice, the soul is supposed to magnify (enlarge, make great) God, not the circumstances. The spirit man is supposed to rejoice, literally *jump for joy*.

This kind of praise defeats the enemy because it releases the powerful spiritual force of joy.

Halal is praise that can be spoken, sung, and instrumental.

Spoken

"Then the Levites . . . stood up to praise the Lord God of Israel with voices loud and high." (2 Chron 20:19)

Sung

"Moreover King Hezekiah and the leaders commanded the Levites to sing praise to the Lord with the words of David and of Asaph the seer. So they sang praises with gladness, and they bowed their heads and worshiped." (2 Chron 29:30)

Instrumental

"Praise him with the sound of the trumpet; Praise Him with the lute and harp! Praise Him with the timbrel and dance; Praise Him with stringed instruments and flutes! Praise Him with loud cymbals; Praise Him with clashing cymbals." (Ps 150:3-5)

Halal is praise that expresses and releases exuberance and joy. In addition to speaking, singing and giving God praise on instruments, we are free to dance.

Dance

Dance is from a root meaning to twist or twirl. The Bible says, "Let them praise his name in the dance" (Ps 149:3). Dancing under the inspiration and anointing of the Holy Spirit is indeed a powerful expression of praise to the Lord.

Zamar

Zamar (zaw-mar) means to *touch the strings or parts of a musical instrument, to play upon* [a musical instrument], *to make music, to sing praises, to sing songs accompanied by musical instruments, to celebrate in song and music.*

The difference between halal and zamar is: halal can be expressed through speaking, singing, instruments, or a combination of singing accompanied by musical instruments. Zamar praise is singing accompanied by instruments, particularly stringed instruments.

Webster's Dictionary defines an instrument as (1) a device for producing music and (2) any object used for making, doing, achieving or promoting something. Some of the synonyms for instrument are tool, implement, utensil, way and means, and moving force.

Zamar praise is a powerful moving force because:

> It creates an atmosphere for the Spirit of the Lord to move.

> The musical instruments themselves can prophesy—that is, express God's heart through notes, chords and melody. Music, played under the inspiration of the Holy Spirit can drive out demonic spirits! (1 Chron 25:1-2; 1 Sam 15:16, 23)

> Zamar praise sets the stage for the prophetic word to come forth—speaking by inspiration of the Holy Spirit to proclaim God's truth. (1 Sam 10:5-6)

> Since the hands are instruments—the fingers themselves are like ten strings—clapping the hands in enthusiastic praise is a powerful, triumphant strike in the spirit against the enemy.

Shabach

There are three aspects to shabach (shaw-bakh') praise. It means (1) address in a loud tone, be loud; shout, praise God; (2) soothe with praises, and (3) still or silence. The first two aspects are what we do; the third is the result.

Address in a loud tone, shout, praise God

"Great is the Lord, and greatly to be praised; and His greatness is unsearchable. One generation shall praise (shabach) Your works to another, and shall declare Your mighty acts." (Ps 145:3-4)

Why would we address God in a loud tone or with shouting? To vehemently praise Him for His greatness, excellence, and mighty acts! The psalmist said: "Make a joyful shout to the Lord. . ." (Ps 100:1), which means to split the ear with sound or to shout for joy!

In the New Testament, we can see an example of a whole multitude of disciples praising the Lord with a loud voice:

"Then, as He (Jesus) was now drawing near the descent of the Mount of Olives, the whole multitude of the disciples began to rejoice and praise God with a loud voice for all the mighty works they had seen, saying: 'Blessed is the King who comes in the name of the Lord.'" (Lk 19:37-38)

With regard to shouting, there are several different

Hebrew words used in the Psalms that mean shout for joy or make a joyful noise or sound.

"... Come before His presence with singing." (Ps 100:2) Singing here speaks of triumphant singing and shouting.

"... Shout to God with the voice of triumph. For the Lord Most High is awesome; He is a great King over all the earth." (Ps 47:1-2)

"... Let us shout joyfully to the Rock of our Salvation." (Ps 95:1)

Soothe with praises

"O God, You are my God; early will I seek You; my soul thirsts for You; My flesh longs for You in a dry and thirsty land where there is no water. So I have looked for You in the sanctuary, to see Your power and glory. Because Your loving kindness is better than life, my lips shall praise You." (Ps 63:1-3)

Still or Silence

"Out of the mouth of babes and nursing infants You have ordained strength [praise], because of Your enemies, that You may silence the enemy and the avenger." (Ps 8:2)

When we praise the Lord with triumphant singing, shouts of joy, and soothing love songs, God is blessed, we are strengthened, and the enemy has to shut his mouth. Praise the Lord!

Barak

> Barak (baw-rak') means *to kneel down, bend the knee, bless (God as an act of adoration), salute, congratulate, praise.*

This form of praise can involve worshipping God on one's knees, laying prostrate with face down, or standing in awe of Him.

Kneeling

Out of approximately 214 times barak is translated bless in the Bible, only three times does it speak of actually kneeling (Gen 24:11, 2 Chron 6:13, and Ps 95:6). Even so, kneeling before God represents the inward bowing of one's heart in reverence, adoration, and submission to Him.

Falling Down or Laying Prostrate

In Revelation, the twenty-four elders, angels, and living creatures fall down and worship the Lamb of God. (Rev 4:10; Rev 7:11)

Standing

> "And the Levites . . . said: Stand up and bless [barak] the Lord your God forever and ever! Blessed be Your glorious Name, which is exalted above all blessing and praise." (Neh 9:5)

The redeemed stand around the throne of God blessing Him with shouts of praise. (Rev 7:9-10)

The key focus of barak, then, is to bless God with all one's heart, with words of love, adoration and praise.

> "... Blessed are You, Lord God of Israel, our Father, forever and ever. Yours, O Lord, is the greatness, the power and the glory, the victory and the majesty; for all that is in heaven and in earth is Yours; Yours is the kingdom, O Lord, and You are exalted as head over all." (1 Chron 29:10-11)

Tehillah

> Tehillah (teh-hil-law), literally *praises*, derives from halal, *to make a jubilant sound*, and elleh, *to rejoice*. Tehillah is a laudation, a hymn, a celebration or exaltation of God, a new song. The corresponding Greek title is Psalmoi (transliterated into English as Psalms) and means *songs*.

There are different kinds of songs. The New Testament speaks of "psalms and hymns and spiritual songs." (Eph 5:19; Col 3:16)

Psalms

A psalm is a song of praise from Scripture set to music. The Book of Psalms is comprised of one hundred fifty different songs of praise.

Hymns

A hymn is a praise song addressed directly to God. It is a celebration of God in song.

Spiritual Songs

A spiritual song is a spontaneous rhythmic song given by the Holy Spirit in one's known language or in a Holy Spirit inspired language. It could also be called a new song. A spiritual song is high praise and very powerful because:

> It is a song that springs out of one's spirit, given by inspiration of the Holy Spirit. It is actually a song from the Lord—fresh from His heart.

> "He has put a new song in my mouth—praise to our God; many will see it and fear and will trust in the Lord." (Ps 40:3)

> God inhabits, literally sits down, dwells in, abides in, and remains in this kind of praise. (Ps 22:3)

Tehillah comes from a heart that is totally surrendered to God. It speaks of a living sacrifice, holy and acceptable to God. It speaks of being full of His Word and His Spirit. The apostle Paul wrote: "Let the word of Christ dwell in you richly in all wisdom, teaching and admonishing one another in psalms and hymns and spiritual songs, singing with grace in your

71

hearts to the Lord" (Col 3:16).

The Word of Christ should feel totally at home in the hearts of Christ believers. In order for the Word to dwell in us richly (abundantly), we must meditate in it day and night, memorize it, speak and do it.

The Word and the Spirit

When one is full of the Word, the Holy Spirit can use the Word to speak to us, to reveal Christ, and to impart wisdom, so we can admonish (advise, counsel, warn) others. "Ever be filled and stimulated with the [Holy] Spirit. Speak out to one another in psalms and hymns and spiritual songs, offering praise with voices [and instruments] and making melody with all your heart to the Lord." (Eph 5:18-19, AMP)

The Holy Spirit's ministry is to glorify Christ. When we are filled to overflowing with the Holy Spirit, the Spirit of pure joy, He will help us to make melody in our hearts to the Lord. Songs should always be dancing around in our spirit just waiting to escape through our lips.

While imprisoned for preaching the Gospel, Paul and Silas prayed and sang praises (hymns) to God. While we do not know what hymns they sang, we know they were very powerful, because "Suddenly, there was a great earthquake, and the prison was shaken to its foundations. All the doors flew open, and the chains of every prisoner fell off!" (Acts 16:25)

How would you like the songs you sing in praise to God to be so powerful they cause an earthquake? The fact is that triumphant Word-based praise expressed through faith-filled Christ believers today has power to shake kingdoms and change spiritual climates for God's glory!

The Hebrew word Shekinah means *abiding presence.* It comes from a root word meaning *to dwell.* When God has an abiding presence in our lives through His Word and His Spirit, we can expect the fullness of His power, love, joy, and peace. "In Your presence is fullness of joy; at Your right hand are pleasures forevermore." (Ps 16:11)

Truly, as our heartfelt praises go up, His glory manifests. When God's Spirit moves, people are saved, healed, and delivered. Zephaniah writes, "The Lord your God in your midst, the Mighty One, will save; He will rejoice over you with gladness, He will quiet you in His love. He will rejoice over you with singing" (Zeph 3:17).

Christ, the Center of our Praise

As we have seen, there are many ways we can express praise to God. Just remember that true praise to God is always Christ-centered. When we minister to God through Christ, He ministers back to us.

We are free to move in the broad spectrum of expressions of praise to the Lord as the Holy Spirit leads. (1 Pet 2:9; 2 Cor 3:17)

As we render triumphant, heartfelt praise to God, we release the glory on the inside. Spiritual yokes are broken, blinders are taken off people's eyes, and lives are changed.

Again, in order for us to flow together and show forth the high praises of God in corporate worship, we must be established as praisers in our homes.

Finally, Jesus Himself said, "in the midst of the church I will sing praise unto thee" (Heb 2:12, KJV). Jesus Christ our High Priest joins in with us and causes our praises to be perfected in the ears of our Heavenly Father. Glory to God! Let Him have His way. Amen.

10

Power of Forgiveness

Throughout the Gospels Jesus Christ teaches His disciples the importance of forgiving others. In His final hours on the cross He prayed for those who crucified Him, "Father, forgive them, for they know not what they do . . . ." (Lk 23:34)

To forgive means *to let go, lay aside, pardon, release.* Whether some wrong done to us or some debt owed to us, we must let it go.

God saved us by His amazing grace and lovingkindness. His forgiveness of our sins is based solely upon the finished work of Christ, not any works we do. However, because God has forgiven us our horrendous trespasses and sins, we have no reason whatsoever to withhold forgiving others for debts owed to us or transgressions committed against us.

Certainly, if we do not forgive others, we will be the ones to suffer spiritually, emotionally, mentally, and even physically. God says, "Be kind to one another, tenderhearted, forgiving one another, even as God in Christ forgave you" (Eph 4:32). As Christ believers, we should maintain a forgiving disposition toward others. As a result, we will have a clear conscience when we ask God to forgive us.

When we forgive others, we release them from the power of their trespass to hold them in bondage. Freely we have received forgiveness from God. Freely we are to forgive others. (Mt 10:8)

Beloved, if you are holding anything against any person, past or present, stop this very moment and deal with the issue.

> Father, forgive me for the sin of unforgiveness. I receive your forgiveness. Just as you have freely forgiven me, so I freely forgive _____. Right now I release _____ from any debt owed to me, real or imagined. I forgive _____ for hurting me. I pray that your mercy, grace and peace will be multiplied to _____.
> In Jesus' Name.

Doesn't it feel good to get rid of unforgiveness? On any given day do not let the sun go down with you holding onto an angry thought against anybody. Let it go. You will be blessed. God says, "Blessed are the merciful for they shall obtain mercy" (Mt 5:7).

11

Prayer Armor

"Stand therefore, having girded your waist with truth, having put on the breastplate of righteousness, and having shod your feet with the preparation of the gospel of peace; above all taking the shield of faith, with which you will be able to quench all the fiery darts of the wicked one. And take the helmet of salvation, and the sword of the Spirit, which is the Word of God; praying always with all prayer and supplication in the Spirit, being watchful to this end with all perseverance and supplication for all the saints." (Eph 6:14-18)

God provides mighty spiritual armor for believers to put on once and for all and keep in place to assure victory in day-to-day spiritual battles. Certainly it is prudent to begin intercessory prayer affirming this spiritual armor. Following is a sample prayer.

Father, in the Name of Jesus, I thank You for establishing me in the Truth. Your Word is Truth. Jesus is the Way, the Truth and the Life; no one comes to You but through Him. Thank You for the Holy Spirit, the eternal Spirit of Truth, who shows me the way into all truth. Lead me in Your path of truth today. (Jn 17:17; Jn 14:6; Jn 16:13)

Father, I purpose to let truth settle and abide in my heart, so that I may think, speak, and operate in truth. Thank You, Lord, for the freedom that comes from knowing Christ and living in the truth of Your holy Word. (Jn 8:32)

Thank You, Father, for the armor of righteousness. I thank You that I am the righteousness of God by faith in Christ Jesus. Thank You for imputing righteousness to me through Christ. Thank You that I have right standing with You and that I am seated in heavenly places in Christ. I declare that Your kingdom of righteousness, peace, and joy in the Holy Spirit rules and reigns in me. (Eph 6:14; 2 Cor 5:21; Eph 2:6; Rom 14:17)

Father, thank You that my feet are shod with the preparation of the gospel of peace. Jesus made peace with You for me through the blood of His cross. I thank You for the good news that because of the work of Christ Jesus at Calvary I now have peace with God and the unsurpassed peace of God, which guards my mind and rules my heart. I thank You that I am anxious for nothing, because I make my requests known to You. (Eph 6:15; Col 1:20; Eph 2:14; Rom 5:1; Phil 4:6-7)

Father, as much as lies within me I will endeavor to live peaceably with all. I will endeavor to be a peace-maker and to minister the gospel of peace as You lead and direct. (Rom 12:18; Mt 5:9; 2 Cor 5:18)

Today, I shall go out with joy and be led forth with peace. Christ is my peace, and I will live, move and have my being in Him. Thank You for keeping me in perfect peace. (Isa 55:12; Acts 17:28; Isa 26:3)

Father, I hold out over all the shield of faith by which I can extinguish all the fiery darts of the evil one. I will walk by faith and not by sight. My faith is totally in You and Your Word. I trust You completely with my life. (Eph 6:16; Mk 11:22; 2 Cor 5:7; Prov 3:3-5)

Father, I receive the helmet of salvation. My spirit rejoices in God my Savior. Thank You for salvation and the deliverance, preservation, safety, soundness, healing, and wholeness I have in Christ. Thank You that Christ has redeemed me from the curse of the law. Thank You, Lord, that as I renew my mind on Your Word, You restore my soul. (Lk 1:47; Gal 3:13; Ps 23:3; Rom 12:2)

Thank You for Your Word, which is alive, powerful, energizing, effective, and sharper than any two-edged sword. Thank You for quickening Your Word to my heart and mind in every situation. By Your Word I will cast down every image, argument and reasoning that tries to exalt itself against the knowledge of Christ. (Heb 4:12; 2 Cor 10:4-5)

Thank You for the Holy Spirit who enlivens me and leads me to pray according to the will of God. In Jesus' Name, I pray. Amen. (Rom 8:11; Rom 8:26-27)

12

Praying the Scriptures

For our prayers to be vitally effective, they should be Scripture based, faith inspired, Holy Spirit infused, and fresh from our hearts to God.

The apostle Paul wrote, "...I will pray with the spirit, and I will also pray with the understanding...." To pray with understanding is most effectively accomplished by praying based on the Scriptures.

The prayers in this chapter are primarily prayers of intercession, prayers for others. Regarding praying for others, the apostle Paul wrote:

> "Therefore I exhort first of all that supplications, prayers, intercessions, and giving of thanks be made for all men, for kings and all who are in authority, that we may lead a

quiet and peaceable life in all godliness and reverence. For this is good and acceptable in the sight of God our Savior, who desires all men to be saved and to come to the knowledge of the truth." (1 Tim 2:1-4)

Personalize these prayers. Make them your own. Shorten them or broaden them. Adapt them to your prayer heartbeat. Each time you pray, do so with freshness, fervency, and faith in God.

Remember, "The eyes of the Lord are on the righteous and His ears are open to their prayers . . . " (1 Pet 3:12)

May grace and peace be multiplied to you for your labor of love.

Leaders in Government

Father, Your Word says the king's heart is in the hand of the Lord and like the rivers of water You turn it wherever You wish. We ask You to turn the hearts of government leaders in _____ to the Lord. (Prov 21:1)

Father, we pray for the Holy Spirit to rest upon the leaders in _____ and make them of quick understanding in the fear of the Lord. (Isa 11:2; Prov 1:7)

We pray for the leaders in _____ to recognize that they have no authority apart from what is allowed by God. May they realize that the Most High God rules in the kingdom of men and gives it to whomever He desires. May they come to know that the true government is upon the Lord's shoulders. (Dan 4:25; Isa 9:6)

We pray for blinders to be taken off their eyes, for the light of the glorious gospel to shine upon their hearts and minds through Christ Jesus. We pray for the Holy Spirit to convince them of sin, and of righteousness, and of judgment. (2 Cor 4:4; Jn 16:8)

Lord, surround them with godly counselors who are full of integrity and wisdom from above. (Prov 11:14; Jas 3:17)

Father, we pray for wisdom to enter their hearts, for knowledge of the Lord to be pleasant to their souls, for discretion to preserve them, and for understanding to keep them, to deliver them from the way of evil, from people who speak perverse things. (Prov 2:10-12)

We pray for the upright and blameless to dwell and remain in government offices, and for the unfaithful to be uprooted from them. For when the righteous are in authority the people rejoice and not groan. (Prov 2:21-22; 20:26; 29:2)

Father, may Your mercy and truth preserve the leaders in _____ and may they uphold their office by loving kindness. We pray for them to lift up a standard of what is right and just. (Prov 20:28; Isa 62:10)

We pray these leaders will put their trust in Almighty God and not in military power and weapons; that they will fear God and not fear mere men. (Ps 46:1-3; Ps 27)

Father, we pray that the leaders in _____ will be filled with the knowledge of God's will with all wisdom and spiritual understanding. We ask these things in the wonderful Name of Jesus Christ, Lord of all. (Col 1:9)

President of Our Nation

Father, "Surely Your salvation is near to those who fear You that glory may dwell in our land." Father, we pray that our President will have a reverential fear of God. We pray that the glory of God will rest upon the President, his family, and the White House, and upon our nation. (Ps 85:9; Prov 1:7)

May Your wisdom enter the President's heart, and knowledge of the Lord be pleasant to his soul. We pray that discretion will preserve him, and understanding will keep him, to deliver him from the way of evil, from people who speak perverse things. (Prov 2:10-12)

Father, we pray the President will not lean on his own understanding but in all his ways will acknowledge You and be sensitive to Your direction. (Prov 3:5-6; Jn 10:4)

Father, we pray You will flood the President's spirit with light, and fill him with the knowledge of Your will with all wisdom and spiritual understanding. (Prov 20:27; Eph 1:17; Col 1:9)

Father, we pray that Your mercy and truth preserve our President and that the President will uphold his office by loving kindness. We pray for him to lift up a standard of what is right and just. (Prov 20:28; Isa 62:10)

Father, we pray that You will preserve the lives of Our President and his family. Surround them with angelic protection so that no foe will gain access to do them harm.

Lord, we pray that You surround our President with godly counselors that You cause to be of integrity and wisdom. And, Father, just as you sent prophets to kings in Bible times to declare the Word of the Lord, send prophets who will gain access to the President and accurately and precisely declare the Word of the Lord. (Prov 11:14; Jas 3:17)

We pray for the President to be of good courage, and know that You shall strengthen the hearts of all who hope in the Lord. (Ps 31:24)

We pray the President will put his trust in Almighty God and not in military power and weapons; that he will fear God and not fear mere men. (Ps 20:7; Ps 27)

Lord, we declare and decree that Jesus is Lord over our President and his family. May grace and peace be multiplied to them, in the Name of Jesus Christ, our Lord.

Salvation for Sinners

(Global prayer for cities, states, nations)

Father, we speak grace to the people of
_____. (Zech 4:7)

We ask the Lord of the Harvest to send laborers to open their eyes and turn them from darkness to light, and from the power of Satan to God, that _____ may receive forgiveness of sins and an inheritance among those who are sanctified by faith in Christ Jesus. (Mt 9:38; Acts 26:18)

Lord, give your ministers the unction and boldness of speech to make known the mystery of the Gospel of Jesus Christ. We pray they will speak and preach not with persuasive words of human wisdom, but in demonstration of the Holy Spirit and power. (Eph 6:19; 1 Cor 2:4)

Father, we declare that every argument, theory, reasoning, and every proud and lofty thing that exalts itself against the knowledge of Christ is cast down, shattered, and destroyed. We declare that the people of _____ are loosed from demonic mind sets and control. We pray that people in _____ will know that Yahweh is God and there is no other. (2 Cor 10:5; 1 Ki 8:60)

Father, send the Holy Spirit to convince the people of sin, and of righteousness, and of judgment. We pray the people of _____ will not resist the convicting power of the Holy Spirit. (Jn 16:8)

We pray that today many people in _____ hear Your voice and are free to believe in and confess Jesus Christ as resurrected Savior and Lord. (Heb 4:7; 1 Thess 1:9; Rom 10:9-10)

Father, we ask that send ministers of the Gospel to establish and encourage the new believers in the faith. We pray that the Word of God will grow, multiply, and prevail in their lives. (1 Thess 3:2; Acts 12:24)

We pray that You will send angels to minister on behalf of these heirs of salvation to keep them safe from hurt, harm or calamity. (Heb 1:14)

Lord, we declare and decree that Jesus is Lord over _____. May grace and peace be multiplied to the people of _____, in the Name of Jesus Christ, the Savior of the world. (Job 22:28; 1 Pet 1:2)

Salvation for Sinners

(Individuals)

Father, we pray that You will send an angel to go before _____ to keep him [her] in the way and to bring him [her] into the place that God has prepared for _____ to hear the everlasting Gospel. (Ex 23:20)

Father, we ask the Lord of the Harvest to send laborers to open the eyes of _____ to turn him [her] from darkness to light, and from the power of Satan to God, that _____ may receive forgiveness of sins and an inheritance among those who are sanctified by faith in Christ Jesus. Lord, surround _____ with strong Christ believers who will positively affect _____'s life. (Mt 9:38; Acts 26:18)

Father, we declare that every argument, theory, reasoning, and every proud and lofty thing that exalts itself against the knowledge of Christ in _____'s life is cast down, shattered, and destroyed. We declare that _____ is loosed from demonic mind sets and control. We pray that _____ will know that Yahweh is God and there is no other. (2 Cor 10:5; 1 Ki 8:60)

Lord, send the Holy Spirit to convince _____ of sin, and of righteousness, and of judgment. We pray _____ will not resist the convicting power of the Holy Spirit. (Jn 16:8)

We pray that today _____ will hear Your voice and is free to believe in and confess Jesus Christ as resurrected Savior and Lord. (Heb 4:7; 1 Thess 1:9; Rom 10:9-10)

Father, send ministers of the Gospel to establish and encourage _____ in the faith. We pray that the Word of God will grow, multiply, and prevail in _____'s life. (1 Thess 3:2; Acts 12:24)

We pray that You will send angels to minister on behalf of _____, an heir of salvation, to keep him [her] safe from hurt, harm or calamity. (Heb 1:14)

Lord, we declare and decree that Jesus is Lord over _____. May grace and peace be multiplied to _____. We ask these things in the wonderful Name of Jesus Christ, the Savior of the world. (Job 22:28; 1 Pet 1:2)

Prayer for Backsliders

Father, we ask You to revive those who once believed, but have turned back from following you. According to Your Word and according to Your lovingkindness, revive the backsliders so they may keep the testimony of Your mouth. (Ps 119:25, 88)

Your Word says, "I will heal their backsliding, I will love them freely, for My anger has turned away from him." Lord, heal broken hearts. Draw backsliders to Yourself with gentle cords of love. (Hos 14:4; Lk 4:18; Hos 11:4)

Lord, send the perfect laborer to them, to open their eyes, to turn them from darkness to light, and from the power of Satan back to God. (Mt 9:38; Acts 26:18; 2 Tim 2:26)

We pray they will awake to righteousness and sin no more. We pray they will seek You with their whole heart. Oh, may they never again wander from Your Word! (1 Cor 15:34; Ps 119:10)

Restore to them the joy of Your salvation, and uphold them by Your generous Spirit. Revive them again, that Your people may rejoice in You! In the name of the Lord Jesus Christ. (Ps 51:12; Ps 85:6)

Restoration of Righteousness

Father, we ask You to forgive our sins and heal our land. (2 Chron 7:14)

Your Word says, "Blessed is the nation whose God is the Lord and the people whom He has chosen for His inheritance." Lord, we declare Your lordship over this nation. We thank You for so bountifully blessing our nation.

Father, we pray that the Word of God will spread and prevail across our nation. We pray for spiritual blinders to be taken off the eyes of the people in this nation and for the light of the glorious Gospel to shine upon hearts and minds through Christ Jesus. (Ps 33:12; Acts 6:7; 2 Cor 4:4)

Father, we pray for a fresh outpouring of Your Spirit upon this nation. We pray for Heaven to rain down righteousness and the earth to open up to receive salvation. We pray that You will cause righteousness and praise to spring forth from our nation before all nations. (Joel 2:28; Isa 45:8)

Father, thank You for Your loving-kindness and tender mercies that are over all Your works. Thank You for protecting this nation from enemies within and without. (Ps 145:9)

The Peace of Jerusalem

Father, we are spiritual watchmen upon the walls of Jerusalem. We shall never hold our peace day or night; we will not keep silent and we will not give You rest until You establish and make Jerusalem a praise in the earth. (Isa 62:7)

You, O Lord, are Israel's shield. Surround Israel with your mightiest angels to keep Israel from harm. (Ps 3:3; Ps 103:20)

We pray that all those who are incensed against Israel and desire Israel's destruction shall be ashamed and confounded, and their plans and strategies against Israel brought to nothing. (Isa 41:11)

We decree that no weapon formed against Israel shall prosper and every tongue that rises in unjust condemnation against Israel shall be shown to be in the wrong. (Isa 54:17)

We pray for the spiritual blinders to be taken off the eyes of the people of Israel, and for the light of the glorious gospel to shine upon their hearts and minds through Christ Jesus. (2 Cor 4:4)

Father, we pray for an outpouring of Your Spirit upon Israel. We pray that You will cause righteousness and praise to spring forth from Israel before all nations. For, "Salvation belongs to the Lord, your blessing is upon Your people." (Joel 2:28; Isa 61:11; Gen 12:3; Ps 3:8)

We pray that You will protect and keep Israel's leaders and government strong.

We say, "O Israel, hope in the Lord; for with the Lord there is mercy, and with Him is abundant redemption. And He shall redeem Israel from all his iniquities." We pray in the name of Jesus Christ, Yeshua ha Mashiach, the Prince of Peace. (Ps 130:7)

An Excellent Husband

Father, I/we stand in the gap on behalf of _____ and declare your Word over his life.

We declare that _____ loves the Lord with all of his heart, with all of his soul, and with all of his strength, and that He seeks first the kingdom of God and God's righteousness. (Deut 6:5; Mt 6:33)

_____ will not seek or receive counsel from the ungodly, nor stand in the path of sinners, nor sit in the seat of the scornful, but his delight is in the law of the Lord, and in Your law he meditates day and night. (Ps 1:1-2)

He is like a tree planted by the rivers of water that brings forth its fruit in its season, whose leaf also shall not wither; and whatever he does shall prosper. (Ps 1:3)

He is a man who excels in his work; he will stand before kings and not unknown men. (Prov 22:29)

He provides for his household. (1 Tim 5:8)

He is rooted and built up in Christ and established in the faith. He walks by faith and not by sight. (Col 2:7; 2 Cor 5:7)

_____ is kind, tenderhearted, forgiving, just as God in Christ has forgiven him. (Eph 4:32)

He is full of the Holy Spirit and wisdom. (Acts 6:3)

_____ has a good testimony among those who are outside. (1 Tim 3:7)

He has left his father and mother and is stuck like glue to his wife. (Eph 5:31)

He is kept from the immoral woman, from the seductress who flatters with her words. (Prov 7:5)

_____ dwells with his wife with understanding, giving honor to his wife, as to the weaker vessel, and as being heirs together of the grace of life. (1 Pet 3:7)

He sanctifies and cleanses his wife by the washing of water by the Word. (Eph 5:26)

He loves his wife just as Christ loves the church and gives himself for her. He loves his wife as his own body. He cherishes and nourishes his wife and renders due benevolence to her. (Col 3:19; Eph 5:25; Eph 5:28-29; 1 Cor 7:3)

He is faithful to God and faithful to His wife. (1 Cor 4:2)

Thank You, Lord, that _____ is an excellent husband.

A Kind, Loving Father

Father, I/we stand in the gap on behalf of _____ and declare your Word over his life. We declare that _____ is full of the Holy Spirit and wisdom. (Ezek 22:30; Acts 6:3)

Because _____ walks in integrity, his children are blessed after him. (Prov 20:7)

_____ knows how to lead and rule his own house well, his children are kept under control and well-behaved. (1 Tim 3:4)

He does not provoke his children to wrath, but encourages them and brings them up in the training and admonition of the Lord. (Eph 6:4)

His heart is turned to and sensitive to his children. (Mal 4:6)

_____ is diligent and provides for his household. (1 Tim 5:8)

Thank You, Holy Father, that _____ is a kind, loving father after your heart, in Jesus' Name.

An Excellent Wife

Father, I/we stand in the gap on behalf of _____ and pray for her and declare your Word over her life. (Ezek 22:30)

_____ fears the Lord, and loves You with all of her heart, soul, and strength. (Prov 31:30; Deut 6:5)

She is virtuous and a crown to her husband. (Prov 12:4)

She has the incorruptible beauty of a gentle and quiet spirit. (1 Pet 3:4)

She adorns herself in modest apparel, with propriety and moderation. (1 Tim 2:9)

She is kind to her husband, tenderhearted, forgiving him even as God in Christ has forgiven her. (Eph 4:31-32)

She is a woman who surrounds, helps, aids, and succors her husband. (Gen 2:18)

_____ respects and honors her husband and is submitted to her husband as to the Lord. (Eph 5:33; 5:23)

_____ has the wisdom that is from above, which is pure, peaceable, gentle, willing to yield, full of mercy and good fruits, without partiality and without hypocrisy. (Jas 3:17)

She is a capable, intelligent and virtuous. (Prov 31:10)

She builds her home through wisdom. (Prov 14:1)

She has the heart and confident trust of her

husband who relies on and believes in her securely, so that he has no lack of [honest] gain or need of [dishonest] spoil. She comforts, encourages and does her husband only good as long as there is life within her. (Prov 31:11-12, AMP)

She girds herself with strength (spiritual, mental and physical) fitness for her God-given task and makes her arms strong and firm. (Prov 31:17, AMP)

She opens her hands to the poor, yes reaches out her filled hand to the needy [whether in body, mind or spirit]. (Prov 31:20, AMP)

Strength and dignity are her clothing. She rejoices over the future, knowing that she and her family are in readiness for it. (Prov 31:25, AMP)

She opens her mouth in skillful and godly wisdom, and on her tongue is the law of kindness [giving counsel and instruction]. (Prov 31:26, AMP)

Thank You, Father, that _____ is virtuous, spiritually, mentally and physically strong, and an excellent wife.

A Kind, Loving Mother

Father, I/we stand in the gap on behalf of
_____ and declare your Word over her life.
(Ezek 22:30)

_____ is full of joy, love, peace; is long-suffering, kind, good, faithful, gentle, and temperate.
(Gal. 5:22-23)

_____ builds her home through wisdom.
(Prov 14:1)

She watches carefully all that goes on throughout her household, and is never lazy. (Prov 31:27)

As a nursing mother, she cherishes her own children. (1 Thess 2:7)

She works with her husband to raise their children in the nurture and admonition of the Lord. (Eph 6:4)

She opens her mouth in skillful and godly wisdom, and on her tongue is the law of kindness [giving counsel and instruction]. (Prov 31:26, AMP)

Strength and dignity are her clothing. She rejoices over the future, knowing that she and her family are in readiness for it. (Prov 31:26, AMP)

Thank You, Lord, that _____ is a kind, loving mother.

Willing and Obedient Children

> "Believe on the Lord Jesus Christ, and you will be saved, you and your household." (Acts 16:31)

Father, as Christ believers, we claim our children's salvation according to Your promise of salvation for our household. (Acts 16:31)

Lord, we thank You that your tender mercies are over our children. (Ps 145:9)

We declare that our children have not been brought forth for trouble, "for they shall be the descendants of the blessed of the Lord, and their offspring with them." (Isa 65:23)

Lord, we pray that our children will flee sexual immortality. We pray they will pursue righteousness, faith, love and peace. (1 Cor 6:18; 2 Tim 2:22)

Father, we say that our children are blameless and harmless children of God without fault in the midst of a crooked and perverse generation, among whom they shine as bright lights in a dark world. (Phil 2:15)

We declare that they are being brought up in the training and admonition of the Lord. Father, we pray that their God-given gifts will be identified and developed. (Eph 6:4; Prov 22:6)

Lord, we declare that "all of our children shall be disciples taught by the Lord and obedient to His will, and great shall be the peace and undisturbed composure of our children." (Isa 54:13, AMP)

We pray their hearts will be turned to their fathers

just as the hearts of their fathers are turned to and sensitive to them. (Mal 4:6)

We declare that our children honor and highly esteem their father and mother and do all things without grumbling or complaining. (Eph 6:2; Phil 2:4)

We believe, and therefore we declare, that our children are increasing in "wisdom and stature, and in favor with God and men." We declare that each of them has an excellent spirit, with knowledge and understanding. (Lk 2:52; Dan 5:12)

Lord, thank You for Your promises.

> God says, "Don't cry any longer, for I have heard your prayers and you will see them again; they will come back to you from the distant land of the enemy. There is hope for your future, says the Lord, and your children will come again to their own land." (Jer 31:16-17, TLB)

Spiritual Leaders

Father, I/we stand in the gap on behalf of Spiritual Leaders. (Ezek 22:30)

Wisdom

Lord, we pray they are filled with the knowledge of God's will in all wisdom and spiritual understanding; that they give themselves continually to prayer and the ministry of the Word; and that they are yielded to and led by the Holy Spirit. (Col 1:9-14; Acts 6:4 Rom 8:14)

Character

Father, may they be blameless, as stewards of God, not self-willed, not quick-tempered, not given to wine, not violent, not greedy for money, but hospitable, lovers of what is good, sober-minded, just, holy, self-controlled. (Tit 1:7-8)

We pray that the elders shepherd the flock of God "serving as overseers, not by compulsion but willingly, not for dishonest gain but eagerly; nor as being lords over those entrusted to them, but being examples to the flock." (1 Pet 5:2-3)

Health

Lord, we pray they are loosed from the power of every sickness, disease, weakness and pain. Thank You, Father, that You have girded them with strength for every battle by the mighty power of the Holy Spirit in their inner man. (Mt 18:18; Isa 53:4-5; Ps 18:29; Eph 3:16)

Protection

Lord, we declare that no hurt, harm, plague or calamity will befall them, and no weapon formed against them will prosper. (Ps 91:1; Isa 54:17)

Home

Father, according to Your Word, the house of the righteous shall stand. (Prov 12:7)

Communication

Lord, may they hold fast the pattern of sound words and preach and teach not with persuasive words of human wisdom, but in demonstration of the Spirit and power. (2 Tim 1:13; 1 Cor 2:4)

Lord, we pray that utterance may be given to them, that they may open their mouths boldly to make known the mystery of the gospel. We pray for the word of the Lord to have free course and be glorified in their lives. (Eph 6:19; 2 Thess 3:1)

Ministry Vision

Father, we pray that they write their God-given vision and make it plain, so that he who reads it may run with it. We pray they are not disobedient to the heavenly vision. (Hab 2:2; Acts 26:19)

Church Services

Father, we pray that the Holy Spirit will be Lord in the church services and assemblies and that the gifts of the Holy Spirit will flow freely as the Holy Spirit wills. Father, thank You for confirming Your Word with accompanying signs and wonders. (2 Cor 3:17; 1 Cor 12:7-11; Mk 16:20)

Supply

Lord, may your spiritual leaders be abundantly supplied according to Your Word which says, "And God is able to make all grace abound toward you, that you, always having all sufficiency in all things, may have an abundance for every good work." In the name of Jesus Christ, Yahweh Yireh, the Lord who sees to it and provides. (2 Cor 9:8)

Traveling Ministers and Missionaries

Prosperous Journey

Father we pray that _____ will have a prosperous journey, that every purpose of the trip will be fulfilled.   Father, thank you that all of _____'s needs will be met according to your riches in glory by Christ Jesus. Lord, we pray that there will be good weather and _____ will have sweet sleep and receive rest and refreshing. (Rom 1:10; Phil 4:19; Prov 3:24; 1 Ki 13:7)

Protection

Father, we declare that Your holy angels, who hearken to the voice of Your Word, will keep _____ in all his/her ways, that no hurt, harm or calamity will befall _____. (Heb 1:14; Ps 103:20; Ps 91:11)

Free course for the Word of God

Father, we pray for a great and effective door to open to _____, and for the Word of the Lord to have free course and be glorified. (1 Cor 16:9; 2 Thess 3:1)

Boldness

Lord, we pray that You will strengthen _____ with mighty power through the Holy Spirit in the inner man and that with all boldness _____ may speak the Word. (Eph 3:16; Acts 4:29)

Wisdom and Spiritual Power

Father, we thank You for the anointing upon

_____to preach the gospel to the poor, to heal the brokenhearted, to proclaim liberty to the captives and recovery of sight to the blind, to set at liberty those who are oppressed, to proclaim the acceptable year of the Lord. We pray that the Lord Jesus will give _____ a mouth and wisdom which all his/her adversaries shall not be able to gainsay or resist. (Lk 4:18-19; Lk 21:15)

Father, we pray that _____ will be full of faith and power and do great wonders and signs among the people, in the Name of Jesus. (Acts 6:8)

Christ Believers

(Body of Christ, the Anointed of God, the Church)

For Babes in Christ

Father, we pray for the spiritual babes in Christ. We pray they will be rooted and built up in Christ and established in the faith. We pray that their hearts will be established with grace, truth, and righteousness. (2 Pet 3:18; 2 Pet 2:1; Heb 13:9; Isa 54:14)

For All Believers

Wisdom and discernment

Father, may every believer be filled with the knowledge of Your will in all wisdom and spiritual understanding. May our love may abound still more and more in knowledge and discernment. (Col. 1:9; Phil 1:9)

Character of Christ

Father, may we all approve the things that are excellent, that we may be sincere and without offense till the day of Christ, being filled with the fruits of righteousness which are by Jesus Christ to the glory and praise of God. (Phil 1:10-11)

Supply

Thank You, Father, that we are ever being filled with the Holy Spirit, with all the fullness of God, the totality and completeness of the gifts, character and anointing of God. (Eph 5:18)

Father, we declare that we live by faith in God. We realize that You are able to make all grace abound toward us, that we always having all sufficiency in all things, may have abundance for every good work. We declare that we lack no good or beneficial thing. (Rom 1:17; 2 Cor 9:8; 1 Thess 4:12)

Endurance

Lord, thank You for strengthening each of us with mighty power through the Holy Spirit in the inner man. (Eph 3:16)

Father, we pray that every believer will fight the good fight of faith and lay hold of eternal life, "For our light affliction which is but for a moment, is working for us a far more exceeding and eternal weight of glory." (1 Tim 6:12; 2 Cor 4:17)

Divine Protection

Father, Your Word says that He who dwells in the secret place of the Most High shall abide under the shadow of the Almighty. Lord, You are our Refuge and our Fortress, our God, on You do we lean and rely and in You do we confidently trust. (Ps 91)

Lord, we are not afraid of sudden terror or of trouble from the wicked when it comes. Your Word says You shall preserve us from all evil. (Prov 3:25; Ps 121:2-7)

We will not be afraid of ten thousands of people

who have set themselves against us. We run to the Name of the Lord, which is our strong tower. (Prov 18:10)

Boldness

Father, thank You that the word of the Lord is sounded forth from believers throughout the earth. Our faith toward God has gone out; and even after we have suffered and been spitefully treated, we are bold in our God to speak the gospel of God. (1 Thess 1:8; 2:2)

> "Now thanks be to God who always leads us in triumph in Christ, and through us diffuses the fragrance of His knowledge in every place." (2 Cor 2:14)

Spiritual Gifts

Father we pray that every believer will make his/her calling and election sure and stir up the gifts of God in him/her. (2 Pet 1:10; 2 Tim 1:6)

Love

Father, thank You for the love of God that has been poured out in our hearts by the Holy Spirit. Lord, we pray that the love of God will be perfected in us. We pray that every believer will increase in sensitivity of heart and love for all people. In the Name of Jesus. Amen. (Rom 5:51 Jn 2:5)

The Severely Persecuted

"Don't forget about those in prison. Suffer with them as though you were there yourself. Share the sorrow of those being mistreated, as though you feel their pain in your own bodies." (Heb 13:3, NLT)

[Pray especially for Christ believers in Afghanistan, Burma (Myanmar), Brunei, China, Cuba, Egypt, Entrea, Ethiopia, India, Indonesia, Iran, Iraq, Libya, Malaysia, Nigeria, North Korea, Pakistan, Saudi Arabia, Somalia, Sudan, Syria, Turkey, Turkmenistan, Uzbekistan, Vietnam.]

Father, pour out Your Spirit in _____ (place). May the light of the glorious gospel of Christ shine in _____ (place) (Joel 2:28; Acts 2:17; 2 Cor 4:4)

May every argument, theory, reasoning and lofty thing that exalts itself against the knowledge of Christ be cast down, shattered, and destroyed. (2 Cor 10:5)

We pray that the spiritual eyes of the persecutors be opened; that they are turned from darkness to light and from the power of Satan to God. (Acts 26:18)

We pray for the heavens to rain down righteousness and for hearts to open up to receive salvation. Lord, may _____ be filled with the knowledge of the Lord, as the waters cover the sea. (Isa 45:8; Isa 11:9)

We decree that ungodly, oppressive laws will be repealed, nullified, or rendered inoperative. (Job 22:28; Mt 18:18)

We pray that the upright and blameless dwell and remain in the land and in positions of authority, but the wicked and treacherous and unyielding to God's Spirit will be rooted out. (Prov 2:21-22)

Lord, look on their threats, and grant to Your servants [the persecuted ones] that with all boldness they may speak Your Word. Stretch out your hand to heal. May mighty signs and wonders be done through the name of Jesus. (Acts 4:29-30)

Father, thank You that the angel of the Lord encamps around those who fear Him, and delivers them. We pray that the persecuted ones will be delivered from destruction. (Ps 34:7; Ps 107:20)

We declare that no weapon formed against them will prosper. (Isa 54:17)

Father, we pray that those persecuted will bless and not curse those who persecute them. (Rom 12:14)

That in God will they put their trust, and not fear what flesh can do to them. (Ps 46:4)

That they will be strengthened with mighty power through the Holy Spirit in the inner man. (Eph 3:16)

Father, we pray they realize that though persecuted they are never forsaken. (2 Cor 4:9; Heb 13:5)

We pray that their needs be met according to God's riches in glory by Christ Jesus. (Phil 4:19)

We pray that prayer without ceasing will be made for the church and especially for our severely persecuted brothers and sisters in Christ. (Acts 12:5)

In the name of Jesus Christ, our Lord. Amen.

Bibliography

Trench, R.C., Synonyms of the New Testament, Ninth Ed. 1880
>   (Grand Rapids, Michigan: Wm. B. Eerdman, 1947, reprint)

Vine, W.E., Expository Dictionary of Old and New Testament Words
>   (Old Tappan, New Jersey: Fleming H. Revell Co., 1981)

Wuest, Word Studies in the Greek New Testament, Vol. 1
>   (Grand Rapids, Michigan: Wm. B. Eerdman, 1955)

Zodhiates, Spiro, Hebrew Greek Key Study Bible
>   (Chattanooga, TN: AMG Publishers, 1991)

Other Books by Capazin Thornton

Keys for Powerfully Effective Intercessory Prayer

10 Keys for Living in Victory Every Day

Prayer Notes:

Prayer Notes:

www.ingramcontent.com/pod-product-compliance
Lightning Source LLC
Chambersburg PA
CBHW060116050426
42448CB00010B/1897

* 9 780097 554730 4 *